A Time for Sharing

Collaborative Ministry
in Mission

A paper prepared
by a working group of
The Mission in England Committee
of the Board of Mission

Board of Mission Occasional Paper No.6

ISBN 0 7151 5533 4

Published 1995 for the Board of Mission of the General Synod of the
Church of England by Church House Publishing.

Cover design by Leigh Hurlock

Printed in England by Bourne Press Ltd

Contents

Preface

I am delighted to be able to commend *A Time for Sharing*. It is a timely contribution to a debate in which the Church must always engage: how in each generation it is to organise itself in mission, to proclaim, witness, and act in loving response to Christian truth.

One of God's gifts to the Church of England at this time is a great sense, in many parishes and dioceses, of the richness and diversity of the skills which are offered in ministry. Learning to use those skills is not always easy, and the enterprise of collaborative ministry makes fresh demands on clergy and laity alike. This paper, from the form of its presentation very clearly a collaborative exercise, offers a range of insights on the theology and practice of ministry in collaboration. The discussion in Parts One to Three is followed by the practical examples given in Part Four. The examples cover urban, suburban and rural areas, religious communities and church plants, and reflect different styles of churchmanship. There is no attempt to conceal the variety in approach, and the differing stages reached, in working out principles which must underpin Anglican ministry in the coming decades.

Those who have contributed to this paper share a common emphasis in their understanding of the Church's mission: that it must use the gifts of all God's people to proclaim to the world the message of God's love. The paper deserves to have wide readership in the Church of England and beyond, and I hope and pray that its message will bear rich fruit.

David McClean

Chairman of the House of Laity

Introduction

In this paper, a working group of the Mission in England Committee has looked at the practice of collaborative ministry between members of the ordained ministry and laity in order to highlight the importance of partnership and sharing. We do this, because we see shared ministry as being crucial to furthering God's mission in the dioceses, deaneries and parishes of the Church of England. We believe that all baptised Christians are implicated in the *missio dei*, the mission of God's love to the world, and that all have particular gifts which may be offered in the service of the Church as part of that ongoing mission of God.

This is particularly important at the present time, not only because the current financial climate is causing hard questions to be addressed in the dioceses of the Church of England, as regards ministry in, and for, mission, but also because rapid changes in our multicultural society require new visions and ways of working in order to bring the Gospel of Jesus Christ into our varied networks and communities. We also believe such sharing to be of the essence of the Church of Jesus Christ. We are encouraged here, to know that the Roman Catholic Church is also looking at collaborative ministry and we believe that we may have much to share ecumenically, as we move forward into an exploration of collaborative ministry in mission.

Rural parishes have for some time been learning that, with their priest living in another settlement, local and therefore lay leadership is essential if their church is to make much headway. In such situations clergy and laity alike are learning to trust each other in sharing the ministry. Such trust does not always come easily.

We are aware that the ongoing discussions about ordained ministry within the Church of England fall under the aegis of the Advisory Board of Ministry and are not the subject of this paper, except where confusions are focused in a blurred distinction between collaborative ministry *per se* and collaborative ministry as we have defined it. Similarly, we are aware that education and training of the laity are properly matters in which the Board of Education has most expertise. However, the importance of *sharing* within ministry has such important mission implications, that it is here that our paper wishes to make a distinctive contribution.

We use 'collaborative ministry' in the understanding that it is a received phrase within the Church, but we also acknowledge that the word 'collaborative' is an ugly term which carries some unfortunate connotations. It has been associated with treachery in war and with informers in the days of apartheid. We are also conscious, as we will show, that the practice of collaborative ministry sometimes carries more of its negative aspects than the positive. But we would like to return to its roots in the Latin *collabore*, meaning 'to work together' and further to extend the concept of collaborative ministry to include not only 'doing' together, but also 'being together', such that collaboration implies true partnership and sharing in a common mission task.

In this paper, we shall attempt to set out a theological foundation for collaborative ministry in mission, within which we shall seek to show some of the reasons why we should all attempt to practice collaborative ministry. We shall follow this with three contrasting perspectives on the practice of collaborative ministry within the structures of the Church of England.

We then go on to provide some perspectives on leadership. Through these, we intend to address questions of continuity, such as what happens to collaborative practice and to mission when an incumbent leaves, or when there is a particular hiatus. We are also required to ask questions about authority and whether collaborative ministry is sometimes misunderstood as a dangerous and threatening strategy, no matter how good a mission tool. We also look at the distinguishing marks of ordination and initiation into mission through baptism and we wish to bring into this the overriding sense of the Great Commission: 'Go therefore and make disciples of all the nations' (Matthew 28:19).

We also provide some descriptive examples of good practice which are known to us and a checklist of pointers for successful collaborative ministry in mission. We also provide a list of resources for those wanting to know more.

The working group has been made up of members of the Mission in England Committee and staff members of the Board of Mission, and includes both ordained and lay persons. It is agreed among us that in commending the practice of collaborative ministry, we ourselves should operate a collaborative process which is as close to the model as we could achieve within the structures. For this reason, we have allowed differing perspectives and understandings to exist, identified, together, but under a common ownership and recommendation. It is hoped that this way of working will illustrate how sharing in respect and courtesy can become an important source of witness, outreach and offering to all people, within the Church and without.

LIST OF WORKING GROUP MEMBERS AND OTHER CONTRIBUTORS

Working Group:

The Revd John Nightingale, Vicar of St Giles, Rowley Regis, Warley, West Midlands (Chair)

The Revd Canon Jesse Sage, Agricultural and Rural Chaplain for Kent

The Revd Richard Oakley, Vicar of Cantley, Doncaster

The Revd Peter Bradley, CME officer Diocese of Liverpool and Rector of Up Holland, Skelmersdale.

Mrs Marion Mort, Mission and Evangelism Secretary, Board of Mission (Secretary to July 1994)

Dr Anne Richards, Mission Theology Secretary, Board of Mission (Secretary)

Other contributors:

The Rt Revd Dr Thomas Butler, Bishop of Leicester and Chairman, Board of Mission

The Revd Canon John Moore, General Director, CPAS

The Revd Canon Robert Warren, National Officer for Evangelism, Board of Mission

Part One

Towards a Theology
of Collaborative Ministry in Mission

God so loved the world

The Revd John Nightingale

God as Trinity

The Christian idea of God is not of a solitary monad needing to create the world with its free and rational beings in order to assuage a loneliness. Instead God is a flow of interlocking energies and relationships. It is through an overflow of God's creative love that the world is created; it is to the dance of love that humankind is drawn, adopted into a new family. The character of God is a model of that perfection to which the Spirit draws us; hence dominance, subservience or isolation are not only immoral but a theological wrong against the God who creates, redeems and sustains us.

The Church as the Body of Christ

Christians are caught up by the Spirit to be part of the Body of Christ, cells of his living presence. As John V Taylor says in chapter 7 of *The Go-Between God*, the primary call of the Church is to be in the right sorts of relationships with God and with one another; out of right being flow right speech and right action. These collaborative relationships involve allowing one another freedom and being ready to sacrifice one's own interests, not out of weakness but out of real respect for others, their needs and gifts, and for the truth.

The World as the Sphere of God's Activity

The world is not a punchbag on which the love of Christ is released through the fist of the Church! Instead it is a place where God the Trinity is already at work. The resurrection of Christ is the assurance that the kingdom of God is really established in the whole world:

'Rejoice the Lord is King . . .'. The mission of Christians is to a large extent to find out what God is doing in the world and to take part in it too. Usually those in the best position to do this are those involved in the part of the world in question, e.g. medical staff, workers in industry or politicians. The role of the ordained is to give them support, resources and questions to help them in this task. For God's activity to be recognised as flesh both sorts of ministry need to be combined. True reconciliation requires heterogeneity or even a community of opposites when people with different backgrounds or experience are not afraid to express themselves, to listen to each other and to try to work through their differences to something better still.

The Ordained Ministry as a Support for all Ministry

As members of Christ's body individual Christians have all sorts of different gifts. Some they may be born with, some develop, others have been thrust by God upon them; some may be with them for a long time, others may come and go. Often individual Christians need help in discerning where their gifts lie. Their own thoughts and feelings may be important but not conclusive evidence; some of them may be too rash, like Peter, and others too fearful, like Timothy. So, from the time when a separate ordained ministry began, one of its functions was to provide oversight and support so that people's gifts might be affirmed, developed or, if necessary, restrained. Bishops, clergy and other authorised ministries such as readers share in this ministry to varying extents today. In this way the gifts of the ordained need the whole body to be of any use; the whole body may not need the gifts of the ordained so immediately, though without them it may be seriously lacking. Those who are ordained should exercise their gifts in concert with their colleagues, ordained and lay, within the Church and outside it.

Collaboration as a continuing process

It is hard to bring in collaborative ministry at a time of crisis. On the one hand desperate times may demand desperate measures; on the other urgency may lead to some scheme being imposed thus negating the very principle of co-operation that collaborative ministry is supposed to stand for. Better for the process to begin when conditions are not too pressing, so that if a crisis does occur, action can be taken readily. Let the collaboration be a matter of principle, not primarily dictated by the saving of time or money.

Collaborative Ministry as a means to security in risk

The prospect of collaborative ministry will excite some and threaten others. The bishop, on behalf of the wider church and other leaders representing him need to be sensitive to the local community, providing the right balance of challenge and reassurance, security and risk. All parties are more likely to be willing to take risks if they are sharing together regularly in a process of mission audit or parish development in which collaborative ministry is an important though not exclusive part; they will also be modelling in their own relationships the collaboration which they are trying to promote locally.

The go-between God

Canon Jesse Sage

We have seen in what John Nightingale has written that the word 'collaborative' can aptly describe our understanding of the nature of God as a Trinitarian relationship of creative love. It can also describe our experience of the nature of the Church as the Community of Faith with the related function of its many individual members (and here we may remember Paul's analogy of the Body, (1 Corinthians 12: 14-31).

To work collaboratively, however, in partnership with others, is of the essence of mission. Indeed, those periods in the Church's history when there have been clear movements of growth and outreach, have nearly always been marked by collaborative styles of witness and ministry (Celtic church, 19th century missions, areas of growth today). In many respects our experience today of the basic principles of growth and movement, by whatever criteria they are measured, is little different from the very early years of the Church recorded in the Acts of the Apostles. It is often through working in partnership that:

> *Initiatives are born*
> *People are empowered*
> *The will of God is discerned*
> *The work is supported and sustained.*

John Nightingale has also referred to *The Go-Between God*, which is the missiological title chosen by John V Taylor to describe the experience of the presence and activity of the Holy Spirit when people work and witness together collaboratively. His plea in 1972, based on the evidence of mission in the Church overseas, is for a restructuring of the Church to encourage this to happen. He says:

> Only in their togetherness can Christians remain alight with the fire of the Spirit. That is the sole purpose of our visible fellowship - to be the fuel upon which the fire is kindled in the earth. The Church must be shaped to carry out that purpose or it will be as frustrating as a badly laid fire. The question we have continually to put to the organisation and structure of the Church is this: Does it bring Christian face to face with Christian in that communion which is the sphere of the Holy Spirit's presence?
>
> (*The Go-Between God*, chapter 7 on *The Evangelical Spirit and the Structures for Mission*)

There are at least four characteristics of the activity of the Spirit, mentioned earlier, associated with the mission of the Church in the Acts of the Apostles:

Initiatives are born

There are a number of instances in Acts where seeds of initiatives appear to have been sown when Christians were meeting together for prayer and fellowship (eg Relief aid for the Church in Judaea 11:27ff; The first missionary journey 13:1ff). Our experience today suggests that it is in the meeting and sharing together of those deeply committed to ministry and mission that the bubble of ideas and initiatives begins to bloom.

People are empowered

The clearest example in Acts of people being empowered and motivated for mission is, of course, the outpouring of the Holy Spirit on the Day of Pentecost. But there are many other examples.

Lack of confidence and courage is the *cri de coeur* of so many Christians who have grown up in our secular society and who have felt intimidated by it. But the situation is changing, secular values are being questioned. The plea so often heard now is for confidence that comes through training. But perhaps the most critical area of training is the experience of collaborative ministry, being empowered and motivated by the experience of learning and sharing and working with others. The book of Acts also seems to suggest that this is so.

The Will of God is discerned

The gift of discernment is one of the more evident activities of the Spirit in collaborative patterns of ministry. Sometimes this may result in new insights, at other times the reshaping of difficult relationships or the correction of errors (eg the Gentile issues at Joppa and Jerusalem 10:44ff).

But the gift of discernment also provides a deeper sense of meaning and purpose and direction to the work to which Christians are called and on which they may be engaged. Indeed, much of the current low morale amongst those who work alone seems to stem from a feeling of having no sense of direction, and of belonging to a Church which has lost its way.

Churches and individual Christians are supported and sustained

As we know from the story of Acts, and from our own experience, a Church which is active in outreach and growth often comes up against unforeseen problems and sometimes meets with strong opposition. Most of us, to be able to cope, require friends and allies to whom we can relate in conversation and prayer and on whom we can depend. The Go-Between God, through partnership and teamwork, is the one who sustains and supports both churches and individuals.

Part Two

Perspectives on Collaborative Ministry in Mission

Providing effective Collaborative Ministry

The Rt Revd Dr Thomas Butler

Theology, need, and personal calling are all converging upon the provision of collaborative ministry in today's church. In theology there is an increasing understanding that all baptised Christians share the one ministry of Jesus Christ. Collaborative ministry, bringing together a range of ministries: lay, ordained, stipendiary, non-stipendiary, liturgical, teaching, pastoral, etc, expresses this understanding of a range of particular ministries within the one ministry of Jesus Christ within His Body, the Church.

Even without this theological insight, the need for collaborative ministry in mission would be obvious. We should not be ashamed to acknowledge the fact that partly our ministry and mission is need-driven, that is: we partly develop new ways of mission by responding to God's 'No' upon present and past ways. For a range of reasons: financial, vocational, structural, sociological, the number of full-time stipendiary clergy has been falling and will continue to fall. Therefore, if the Church of England is to maintain a nation-wide parochial system (which I would argue is still the best way of maintaining ministry in difficult as well as comfortable areas), then the ordained, stipendiary ministry must be complemented and enhanced by other forms of ministry, and ways of collaborating must be developed. Then, further, one of the most positive factors about church life in our generation is the reality that very many individual lay men and women have felt called to exercise a direct ministry in and around their local church in addition to the traditional calling of the lay Christian to exercise a faithful ministry at work or home.

This convergence of theology, need, and calling has led to an explosion of lay ministries which in turn has raised questions about training, accountability, and collaboration. Training is probably the easiest problem to solve. The traditional place for lay people to be trained in ministry is the local parish church and the trainer has traditionally been the vicar. Sunday School teachers, youth leaders, and so on, have been provided in this way for generations, with additional training resources being increasingly supplied by the diocese or by Christian organisations. Much training for today's wide variety of lay ministries is still so provided, particularly in the large parishes, but we have also seen the development of ambitious diocesan training programmes. These are needed in order to provide lay people in every parish, large or small, with the opportunity of responding to a call to minister, but they are also of great value to those worshipping and witnessing from the base of a large church of a single tradition in opening their eyes to a wider theological, missiological and ecclesiological perspective.

There are problems with training programmes taking place beyond the parochial level, however. A common frustration has been experienced when lay people attend particular courses of training, emerge full of enthusiasm, and then find that the local clergy or lay leadership do not want to make use of their ministry. It would not be wise to leap to the conclusion that this is due to the conservatism or fear of the traditional leadership. It might be that the lay persons concerned, whatever their own feelings, are not called to a particular ministry even though they have been trained for it. The biblical understanding of ministry is that a personal call from God is then to be tested by the Church. We have such a pattern of testing the call to ordination, and some such test seems to be needed at least for some of the ministries exercised by lay people in their local church. Some training courses have developed a kind of two track approach to training programmes. Of these, some, educational and theological, are open to everyone who wishes to enrol. Others, pastoral and practical, are open to those coming with the encouragement of their local church, with a clear understanding that there will be the opportunity of exercising the particular ministry when training is completed.

The difficulties of providing training for lay ministries should not be over-estimated, however. Mostly the experience is positive and an indication of this is how much most dioceses are investing in such programmes and courses. The most flexible of these enable a lay person to enrol for a particular piece of training (eg bereavement visiting), but also encourage enrolment in some kind of general Ministry Foundation

Course. Following this, particular pieces of training or education can be pursued in greater depth, or the way can be opened for training for more formal or accredited ministries such as licensed lay reader or non-stipendiary ordained ministry (NSM). Not surprisingly, the experience is that once people have exercised one form of ministry, they find this so fulfilling that they want to offer themselves for training for more demanding ministries: the person who first reads a lesson in church, experiences a later call to become a licensed lay reader; the person who first spends a morning a month visiting a ward in the local hospital, experiences a later call to train for hospital chaplaincy. This natural pattern lies behind the concept of the local ordained ministry as it has been developed.

Initial training for a variety of ministries, then, is relatively straightforward. What is far more difficult is the training of the stipendiary clergy both to welcome and make use of the wealth of talent available. Many pay lip-service to collaborative ministry in mission, but it is the experience of most bishops and archdeacons, that 'making it happen' still seems to be going against the natural grain of many clergy and local church people. A young priest can go right the way through an enlightened programme of training at theological college and in post-ordination, in which the need for collaborative ministry is emphasised again and again. Still, some five years after ordination he or she will come to the bishop and say 'I think I'm ready to run my own parish now'. Nor is the situation any better when the priest is ordained in later life. It might be thought that such a person, having worked in a team situation in another profession, would be far more open to collaborative ministry within the church. Not a bit of it. Just because the priest knows the demands which are made upon those working in team situations, there is a yearning for the simple one-vicar-and-his-cure ministry of yester-year. But of course such ministry is increasingly disappearing for financial and structural reasons and, whether against the grain or not, clergy are having to come to recognise that their ministry must be within a wider collaboration. Local lay people also need help in understanding and welcoming this new pattern of ministry.

Providing initial and in-service training in collaborative ministry for clergy, together with educating local lay people in the realities of Christian ministry in our generation is one of the major challenges facing the church today. It has to stem from the culture of a diocese, and it must include the provision of consultants to be available for parish teams who have developed this pattern of ministry. It would be wrong to give the impression that such ways of ministry are easy, - they are not. A vicar changes, there is a clash of personalities, there is a clash of mission or spiritual insights, a person burns out, a person returns from a Summer programme exploding with enthusiasm – all these things can put strain upon a previously well-running team, and without the aid and advice of an external consultant it can be tested to destruction.

All of this also emphasises the need for there to be clear expectations from the outset. For ordination and for licensed lay-readers, clear procedures have been developed for selection, training, in-service appointment and accountability. Some of these traditional procedures have now become more varied (eg in the appointment of a new vicar to a parish, and his relationship to the lay leadership in the parish), but in general the procedures are relatively clear and therefore room for misunderstanding is limited. This is the not the case for the proliferation of lay ministries which are now to be found in the church. The question of someone emerging from a course of training to find that their ministry is not welcome in their local church has already been mentioned, but the potential problems are far wider than this. For example:

> How is a 'lay elder' or 'lay pastor' or 'lay evangelist' selected?
> How long does such a person serve?
> How does he or she lay the ministry down?
> How is the ministry accredited (at parish, deanery or diocesan level)?
> What happens if the person moves to another parish?
> To whom is the minister accountable?
> How does a ministry team relate to the Parochial Church Council or Churchwardens?

The experience is that it is far easier to start leadership teams, or to start an individual exercising a ministry, than it is to sustain the team or the person for a long period of creative ministry. It may be that the Church of England can learn from other denominations such as the Methodist Church who have trodden this path earlier (with not total success). We certainly need to be on a sharp learning curve if we are to avoid difficulties and disasters.

Collaborative ministry in mission is here to stay. It is a gift of God to our generation. But it is no fast track to the establishment of the kingdom of heaven. We will need to think clearly and plan carefully if it is be the sharp weapon in the Church's armoury of mission that many of us believe it to be.

A view from the grass roots

Dr Anne Richards

'Collaborative styles of ministry...refers to clergy and laity working together in the ministry of the Church. This century has seen a great expansion in the role of the laity in the Church's ministry, an expansion that many would hold to be a recovery of an essential New Testament principle'. *Team and Group Ministries* 1985, p.1 [2]

In the previous section, Bishop Tom Butler drew attention to questions surrounding the training for, and exercise of, collaborative ministry in mission. This section draws on research among parishes all around the country, across a variety of situations and churchmanship. The purpose of the research was to ask clergy and laity in these situations how they operated collaborative ministry, what theological rationale (if any) they employed, what actually went on in practice and how they felt about the workings of such relationships. A number of common themes emerged as well as a set of common difficulties and joys. The research has been shared among them and further reactions and thoughts obtained. What follows attempts to draw out some of the most common ideas and feelings and attempts to give these some context and structure. However, the material has been drawn from first-hand experience at the parish level, and as such is referred to as 'grass roots' experience.

Clergy

Seen from the grass roots, a stipendiary member of the ordained ministry comes from the wider church as an 'apostle' into a local situation. Such a person may 'interface' with the local congregation who have no experience of church other than their own parish. The incumbent may offer detachment, vision, and complementary perspectives of parish needs. In particular, the strongest factor in bringing about collab-

orative ministry may be the vision of the parish priest. This is necessarily not a short term vision, but a prophetic strategy. A vision of
restoration and regeneration may put collaborative ministry in mission
in tandem with external improvements in the local environment and
church life and empower a congregation to become a missionary people.
Consequently, collaborative ministry should not be seen as compensa-
tion for a lack of stipendiary clergy, but as expressive of the move
towards wholeness and in an understanding of the Kingdom. The
success of collaborative ministry where vision is a sustaining factor may
mean that the incumbent needs to stay with that community for a meaningful period, or otherwise face the problem of enabling others to
sustain a vision. Continuity and stability are often seen to be paramount,
if the vision is not to fade or to be lost altogether.

While in principle, this points to an ideal partnership between clergy and
laity, the practice is rarely ideal. First, clergy may conspire, consciously
or unconsciously, to keep congregations in a state of cosy unawareness
of their potential as part of a need to maintain control. This may happen
even where collaboration does in fact exist. Indeed, the system of
appointment, the bringing of the wider church into the local can also be
perceived as the bringing of an innate authority which in itself abrogates
collaboration. Some members of the laity explained that even though
they had lived, worshipped and ministered in their community all their
lives, there was still the assumption that a new incumbent coming into
their church would have 'the authority of the answers' for their community because this was what he or she had been called, selected and
trained for. Such local people felt they could not offer a useful collaboration where they were overshadowed by the institutional weight of the
church which suggested so strongly that the incumbent's training, gifts
and experience were 'right' for them. This is particularly clear where
clergy operate the kind of 'management' model of collaborative
ministry which tends only to seek to maintain the status quo and is not
enabled for mission.

Further, Team or Group ministries may actually mitigate against partnership, placing collaborative emphasis on incumbents and relegating
the laity to 'assistants' and 'helpers'. Feeling from the grass roots often
emphasises that clergy teams can de-skill the laity by strengthening
power and providing a united front of decisions; therefore what is called
collaborative ministry may, in fact, be no such thing, especially where

there is tacit understanding that the clergy are permanently in control and the inevitable final arbiters. Where incumbents stand in guardianship or parental oversight of the laity, shared ministry may be compromised, with the clergy feeling vindicated when things go wrong and bewildered when things go right. For clergy, collaborative ministry may mean living on the edge, being marginalised, giving away authority. But this can be dangerous: empowerment may mean giving up one's own power and living on a critical edge in humility. This may lead to a feeling of meaninglessness in clergy who cannot reappraise for what they were trained and selected, or conversely, lead to a need to respond to the increased authority and critical demands of the laity by setting themselves extremely high (or even impossibly high) standards. Several incumbents spoke of feeling deeply challenged by excellent lay-led worship, pastoral care and by other lay groups. One incumbent felt the need to study vigorously in order to produce superlative sermons; another felt he had nothing he could say that would add anything meaningful.

Laity

It should be emphasised that all people are equipped to minister to others and that intuitive, pastoral and prayerful ministry goes on in various ways within the Body of Christ and within the wider world also. This may be seen particularly where there is a Church Centre which relies on the help and ministry of specialists whose gifts of time and experience are part of the collaborative ministry even though they may not be part of the church life or even Christian. For example, one Church Centre was given superb service from an atheist social worker; another by a person giving sensitive and careful financial advice, who nonetheless was not a Christian.

However, collaborative ministry at the grass roots begins from a recognition that 'Baptism does therefore include an authorization to minister as a Christian' (Tiller, p.66 [116]). All baptised Christians therefore are ministers and witnesses of the Church, whose potential may be recognised in various ways. The structures of the Church allow, for example, for Locally Ordained Non-Stipendiary Ministry (LNSM), where a corporate sense of vocation from the parish is channelled into the individual who must internalise and own it. *Faith in the City* has pointed out that LNSM may have an important function as reconciler between

16

church and community. Laity may also be formally trained for ministry, as Lay Readers or Pastoral Assistants. They may also belong to the formal structures of the church as officers of their parish church. In other cases, there may be informal groups or teams of lay people offering ministries. Some may have had local training, some may not.

There appears now to be a general consistency of lay participation in eucharistic worship where the adoption of Rite A over the Book of Common Prayer gives the laity more opportunities to contribute to the wholeness of worship. Non-eucharistic worship may be entirely lay-led, and they may own the worship so completely that they reject styles of worship preferred by the clergy. It is however noted that, paradoxically, prescribed liturgical patterns often give more freedom, and prevent the clergy moving in to oversee the worship and thereby reasserting power.

Laity may be trained to assist with marriage preparation and bereavement visiting (eg using *Marriage in Mind*, Church Pastoral Aid Society; *Living with Loss*, also CPAS) and in baptism and confirmation preparation, for example using *Hands On* (National Society/CPAS). Laity may take on visiting and the administration of sick communion as well as being responsible for the prayer life of the parish. Laity may also take on the day to day administration, often through a parish secretary or by a team producing the parish magazine. In multi-parish benefices, a co-ordinator or central person may be an important focus of psychological security when the clergy are on the move around a very large geographical area. Finance may be handled independently by the laity, and they may also represent the church on outside committees or within activities which blur the distinction between church and community life. If collaboration between clergy and laity is channelled through the structures of the church, then the office of churchwarden may come into its own and in some cases this has been the fruitful source of LNSM. Activation of the Parochial Church Council from rubber stamp to proper policy-making body may be particularly important, allowing traditional roles and offices to be extended into other ministerial roles without disturbance. It is also especially noticeable that in crisis situations, laity are effective in keeping the life of the church going and may at critical times discover gifts and abilities that may otherwise have been completely dormant. These examples highlight the great potential for mission and ministry which all congregations have. Conversely, they also expose the danger of introversion, such that the ministerial possibilities are directly only in and to the local church and not to the wider world. It is important that part of the collaborative process includes an understanding that mission through ministry is to the wider church and indeed the whole world.

The structures and collaborative ministry

Collaborative ministry may contain the underlying assumption that as the priest is 'central' so the laity should be drawn in to share in his or her centrality. However the very marginality of the laity in terms of the difference between their and the clergy's daily lives, is an important factor in collaborative ministry in mission. Similarly, there can be a tendency to see NSM and LNSM as being lower orders of clergy, especially where selection and training ignores their local experience. This local experience needs urgently to be upheld and affirmed by the wider church and acknowledged as a *lack* by the stipendiary clergy. A corollary to this point is the difference of language use by the clergy and by the laity. If collaborative ministry means passing on an 'insider' language to the laity, this imputes a very different connotation to accreditation and risks alienating the laity from the ordinary world. It implies urgently that clergy become sensitive to the discourse of the laity and through collaborative ministry, allow that discourse to inform the Church. Prayer too, should be seen to be a shared foundation for a corporate spirituality sustaining the local church in the context of the wider church. There can be no collaborative doing without collaborative being, yet many clergy conceal their own spiritual journeys and prayer lives from their people.

A particular problem which ensues is that of commitment. It is clear that it is necessary to discern the parameters between 'interest' and 'commitment'. Forcing people who show the former into the latter can have serious repercussions, whereas the committed can sometimes be found to overcommit themselves to the detriment of jobs and families. There is seen to be a tension between the voluntary nature of the laity's ministry and the stipendiary clergy, and because the laity are volunteers they may ask questions about the clergy's role or may be unable to find ways of sustaining commitment if enthusiasm suddenly wanes. The gap between interest and commitment can often be seen in church planting situations, where the committed team moves off to the plant, leaving the planting church with a sense of bereavement and a need for the clergy to fill the gap and to discern interested people for nurture into ministry. The sustaining vision and stability of clergy can be particularly important here. Another problem with commitment may be the influence of outside factors, such as the facility of owning a car or having flexible working hours. In rural areas, where journeying is fact of working life and ministry, these kinds of factor may become crucial.

Loyalty and responsibility are also important in good collaborative ministry. The point at which an incumbent leaves can be disastrous for collaborative ministry, for the loyalty of a team, as chosen from within a partnership, is not always easily transferred to the incoming incumbent, no matter how committed personally to collaborative ministry. This points up too, how important it is to distinguish exactly where decisions and decision-making lie. There is always the possibility that collusion can begin to operate at PCC level, cutting off the larger congregation and mitigating against sharing on behalf of that congregation. Conversely, even where the incumbent has surrounded him or herself with 'yes people', that incumbent can still become the scapegoat for bad decisions if responsibility is not seen and understood to be shared. In other situations, where power has previously been badly exercised, collaborative ministry can be the agent of healing and of mobilisation for mission. Sometimes the lack of an incumbent can identify a 'priest-shaped gap' which makes clear the parameters of the collaborative partnership and lays down the need for a leader whose discernment and gifts for enabling people can enrich and empower the church. John Moore will discuss this in a further section in this paper.

Finally, collaborative ministry between clergy and laity has immediate pastoral significance, but it also has significance for networking beyond the parochial boundary and for ecumenical partnerships and working. Collaborative ministry in mission does not just require vision and discernment between incumbents and people, but the experience is also that people automatically get on and work together ecumenically. There is consequently a larger grass roots effect of promoting reconciliation and unity, where collaborative ministry is effective.

Finding new structures for ministry

Canon Robert Warren

One aspect of collaborative ministry which needs engaging is the development of new structures for church life which will facilitate the church's mission in a post-modern culture. There are profound changes taking place in society, as our culture moves beyond the Christendom/Enlightenment worldview in which we currently operate. In such a setting the Church needs to find new ways of being church.

Two particular, and related, changes have considerable significance for the life of the church. First, people relate increasingly within networks rather than relate geographically. They relate to people 'most like them', rather than 'nearest to them'. Indeed, one hundred years ago, the question 'who are you closest to?' would almost invariably have drawn the response of naming the neighbours. It is that geographical basis for relating that has found expression in the parish structure (see figure 1).

Figure 1

geographical

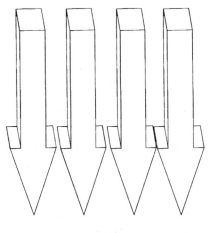

parishes

However, today, we need to adjust to the fact that there is a sociological perspective to be overlaid on that pattern (figure 2). It produces networks of relationships.

Figure 2

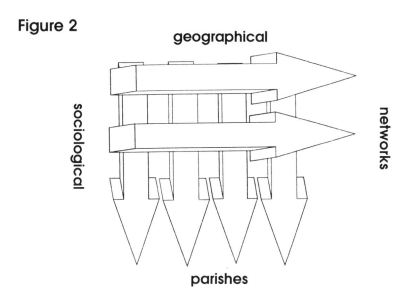

geographical

sociological

networks

parishes

Such an approach has significant parallels with the way the Celtic church evangelised 'people-groups', whilst the more static Roman approach produced fixed 'patches' or 'parishes' for approaching gatherings of people. In today's complex society both patterns need to continue; it is not that one should be replaced by the other.

Second, people now inhabit several different 'worlds' which function like sealed units. Whilst people in medieval times, and until comparatively recently, operated in one world in which each network of relationships was built on the succeeding one (see the concentric circles of figure 3), people today function in disconnected ('dis-located'?) communities (figure 4).

Moreover, the mosaic of 'worlds' in which people live is overlaid with a mosaic of cultures. Graphically this could best be illustrated by a three-dimensional noughts-and-crosses game. It means that those people to whom others feel nearest will be the fellow- 'greens', 'yuppies', 'executives', 'gays', or 'underclassers', etc.

Even though there is a major return to the rural areas, this does not mean that people are going back to what was, but rather on to something new. Each parish church is set in a geographical area in which different groups function in various, and often sharply differentiated, people-groups.

I believe that the task of the church is to engage with such groups.

Like the Base communities of South America, members of such a post-modern culture are likely to be drawn more easily to the church functioning on a kind of horizontal axis ('Word-laity'), rather than on a vertical axis ('Priest-sacrament') as outlined in Leonardo Boff's book, *Ecclesiogenesis* (see figure 5).

Figure 3

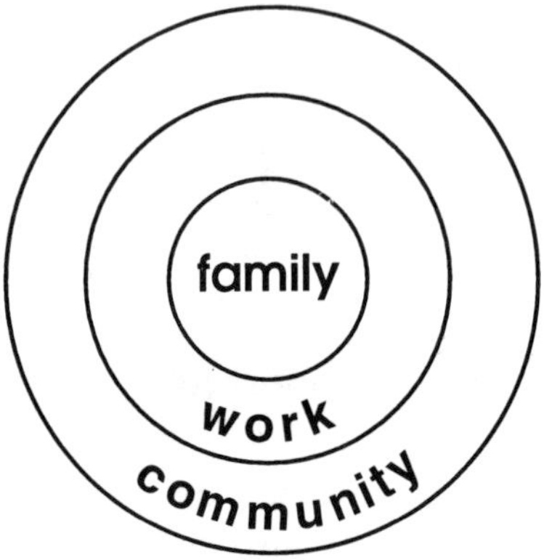

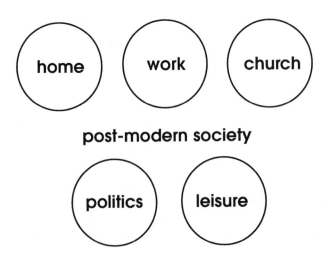

pre-industrial society

Figure 4

post-modern society

Figure 5

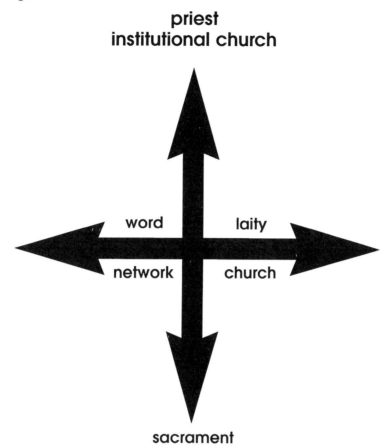

**priest
institutional church**

word   laity

network   church

sacrament

This could well lead to a more energised church, collaborative in the whole of its life, not just in its leadership structures, built on an awareness of baptism as the ordination of the laity (see *Faith in the Countryside*). In such a grouping people are likely to function as 'employees' of the church (actively working at creating community and participating in mission) rather than as consumers (coming, in the double sense, for the services on offer).

Larger parish groupings, with lay and ordained collaborative-style leadership teams, are likely to enable the church both to maintain traditional parochial structures, and develop new models of being church alongside them.

These new structures will be network-type expressions of the Christian faith, functioning with very light and fluid structures. They are likely to be almost entirely 'self-servicing', like the 2,500 members of Alcoholics Anonymous in the UK who function without any buildings, or paid (full-time, or part-time) employees.

Collaboration will be vital to finding such new ways of being church in a post-modern culture. Clergy and laity will need to exist alongside the traditional expressions of institutional Christianity. Some will function clearly from within the parish structure, some will be more loosely affiliated, and yet others will be unconnected. Others may start entirely separate and move, in different stages, to the point where they become a new form of parish church.

Such groupings can already be observed on the church scene in the UK today. Holy Disorder and Oxford Youth Works are working among young people, and church planting (now happening nationwide at around one new congregation planted per fortnight, see *Breaking New Ground: Church Planting in the Church of England*) is demonstrating how churches are reaching out to underchurched areas. These are all ways in which expressions of the faith in new forms of community life are bubbling to the surface. They all involve, and need, collaborative styles of leadership and functioning. It is also vital that the existing church welcomes and works with such developments. We must avoid entering into competition out of a desire to control. Collaboration between 'existing' and 'new' forms is vital to both. However, now surely, is the time to let a thousand flowers bloom.

Part Three

Leadership

Styles of leadership

Canon Robert Warren

If new structures for the mission of the church are to emerge there will need to be a matching change in the church's understanding and practice of leadership within the ordained ministry. I believe that leadership for collaborative ministry in mission is likely to be along the following lines:

Being a conductor rather than director

Leadership for collaborative ministry in mission will involve identifying the gifts of those within the local church, and seeking to harmonise their individual (and sometimes idiosyncratic) contributions. The conductor is the one person in an orchestra who does not play an instrument. Too easily the local church has been built around the gifts of the incumbent. What will be needed will be the building of churches around the rich mosaic of gifts, insights and convictions of the whole of the laity. For this to happen, the ordained minister will need to affirm, train and support such gifts as well as, where necessary, confront the hidden power agenda that may be shaping what is going on.

Becoming a facilitator rather than a provider

I believe leadership will need to avoid the disempowering style of the provider/client relationship. As such it will need to enable people to 'do it themselves'. In this way the Church can be prophetic by the very way in which it operates. In so doing the Church can model for society a better way of doing things than the too frequent way of the professional classes taking power and decision-making away from people. Such a change of style may well uncover insecurity in the ordained clergy which will need to be owned and dealt with.

Permission-giver rather than permission-witholder

I believe leadership will need to discover ways of both affirming lay involvement and encouraging lay initiatives in the whole of life. Collaborative ministry in mission involves going beyond allowing the laity to do what the priest has traditionally done. It is about allowing the laity to shape and to be the initiators, of both their ministry and that of the clergy.

Steering rather than rowing

I believe leadership will need to learn, and practise, a style of operating which moves beyond 'doing everything' into 'causing everything to be done'. Delegation is a crucial part of this style, but again it will be more than giving the laity the jobs the vicar wants them to do. It will include discovering the vision and convictions of the laity with a view to helping facilitate that direction.

Being a person rather than a parson

I believe that the primary sense in which a priest is an icon, or representative, of Christ, is in being reflections of his humanity: the incarnate Jesus. In this sense, being human is what Christianity is all about. The leaders need therefore to own and articulate their own sense of meaning, discovery of wholeness, and escape from addictions. Personal openness to change and growth, and the vulnerability associated with such openness will be essential for such a living out of the Gospel.

Leadership and organisation

Canon John Moore

Given that collaborative ministry – or working together, to use a less complicated phrase – is a necessary part of Christian ministry-in-mission at every level, the question arises as to how this working together can actually be organised and co-ordinated. Clearly no member of a team, however loosely that team holds together, can do just what he or she wants without reference to its effect on the others and to the task in hand. Thus a co-ordinating function is vitally necessary if genuine teamwork is to be a reality.

Further, this function at any one time needs to be vested in one person. This person's contribution to the team is, humanly speaking, the key to effective collaborative ministry in mission. This is not saying that this person is exalted to a status above the others, but it is saying that teams need someone whose role can ensure that agreed actions are done, that there are clear lines of accountability, that the whole team is properly pastored and so on. The leader may well be at his best when the people say 'we did it all ourselves', as Robert Warren has previously shown, but the leader is there in the first place. It is sometimes said that in order for people to contribute effectively in a shared task they need to know clearly:

> what it is they have agreed to do
> who they are accountable to
> how they are getting on
> where they go to for help in getting better

The person who ensures these things happen is the leader.

Some find this difficult and out of step with the way things ought to be done in the Church. The New Testament does not appear to agree with them. If the model pursued by the early Church as it organised itself for worship and mission was the model of the synagogue, we know from the New Testament that the people were not only overseen by elders, but that there was a 'chief of the elders'. Also, later, Peter takes up the theme of the ordering of the Church by talking about the elders as shepherds. All would have known that the word shepherd meant 'leader' and would have known from their history and from their understanding that their chief shepherd was Jesus himself, and would surely have come to the notion that one of them would have to act as chief shepherd in any given locality.

At an anecdotal level, the most effective churches I have seen have been where there is strong collaborative ministry. But, this has only happened because there is quality leadership behind it. The fact that leadership is focused in one person has ensured people know what the team's task is and has enabled them to achieve it. They act as what someone once described as 'agents of coherence and purpose'. That seems a good definition.

If collaborative ministries for mission are to be effective then a great deal of effort will be needed to help people to become quality team leaders having all the skills of a chief shepherd and all the humility and attitude of a humble servant. The non-church world may have much to teach us here.

Providing leadership from a catholic perspective

The Revd Richard Oakley

I have found this section extremely difficult to write, not because I do not believe in collaborative ministry in mission, but because of assumptions that tend to be made about it. The very phrase 'collaborative ministry' has become associated with a certain ecclesiology and theology of ministry which does not tie in with a more traditional, catholic, theology and practice within the Church of England. Those of us in that tradition sometimes find ourselves in difficulty because, for instance, we are criticised for not training people in a particular and narrow form of that ministry. Perhaps another difficulty is that, where collaborative ministry (in whatever form) does operate in a catholic parish of the Church of England, it takes a less self-conscious form which arises directly from the life and worship of the congregation, rather than trying to impose what seems to me to be alien ways and structures upon it. This section does not set out a theology or model of collaborative ministry in mission but questions some of the assumptions about it.

God

It is God who provides both the content and the context of our mission. As my fellow contributors have shown elsewhere in this paper, the Holy Trinity provides an obvious model for the Church in terms of community. But the very nature of the Trinity is always to be outgoing. This is seen in the very act of the creation itself, and the love of God is forever reaching out into the whole of creation. It also seeks to draw us into an ever deeper participation in that communion of love which is God. Our mission also has to have that twofold action of reaching out to where the love of God already is and seeking to draw others into communion.

In that divine action I would also wish to highlight the particular and central form that it took in the Incarnation. In Jesus Christ we see that reaching out in total self-giving, that we might share in the divine life and communion of which the Church is the concrete sign: 'I, if I am lifted up, will draw all men to myself' (John 12:32). But God has also taken the very great risk of making frail human beings indispensable to his mission of love to the world. In thinking out the theology and practice of collaborative ministry for mission, then, the relationship of Jesus to, and with, his disciples is particularly important.

Worship

In considering some of the models of collaborative ministry in the service of mission, we are faced with certain inherent difficulties. One of these concerns the structures we have in the Church of England and especially how people relate to each other within those structures. Similarly, whatever the shape of the structures, the picture which is presented seems inevitably to draw a sharp demarcation between the Church and the world, and to present such structures as static and without that essential dynamism which is part of the nature of God. A better illustration, for me, is that of a centre from which all else radiates out, like the spokes of a wheel from a hub, or the point at which a stone enters a pond and from which the ripples move out. That central point has to be God and our worship of him and in the catholic tradition, that worship is primarily in the eucharist, so the altar symbolises that originating, focal point.

I believe that one of the primary reasons for our existence as human beings is so that we may choose to exercise our ability to worship God. We believe the mission of the Church will be complete at the parousia, but the worship of God will never cease. Whatever our individual tasks, then, within the mission of the Church, it is within the eucharist that we come to proclaim our communion and, implicitly, collaboration with one another and with God. It is from this central point that we are sent into the mission of the Church in the whole of our daily lives 'to live and work to his praise and glory' and it is to this central point that we return to offer together that same mission in thanksgiving. (An illustration of how the eucharist is seen as this focus of mission in a particular parish can be found in *The Gospel and Our Culture: Good News in our Times*, p.86). I also believe that the mission of the Church must include the drawing of people to the worship of God, such that the eucharist then demonstrates that twofold missionary action to which I have referred. Since Vatican II, the eucharist is also now seen as a corporate, collaborative event in which everyone participates, though some may have particular tasks within it. While celebration of the eucharist is reserved to the presiding priest, lay people who are eucharistic ministers, lectors, intercessors, those involved in the ministry of welcome and in the music are all part of the visible collaboration, while those who clean the church, prepare the linen, type the notices or arrange the flowers also collaborate in the common mission aim of the worship. At this focal point of collaborative ministry in mission we may be aware of both visible and invisible ministries at work. Here, collaboration involves difference of function, but equality of intention: it is not that the reserved ability to celebrate the eucharist or the ability to administer the chalice or read lessons is more 'important' than flower arranging, but that each of these actions represents a part of the common offering.

The Church

Some of us are profoundly disturbed by trends within the Church which seem to imitate questionable features of the world at large. One of these is the creation of organisations and structures which are all too often dehumanising. Too many of these are concerned with profit and management rather than with people. Many people believe that an important aspect of the Decade of Evangelism should be the evangeli-sation of structures, but if this is to happen the structures of the Church must also be challenged and transformed. There is a great danger, then, of identifying a need for new structures to facilitate collaborative ministry for mission, which, with all the best intentions, end up becoming so time and energy consuming that this enterprise inhibits rather than promotes the mission of all God's people. We need to free people from structures rather than create new ones so that they are freed to live and to proclaim the Gospel in the whole of life: 'For the Church, evangelising means bringing the Good News into all the strata of humanity and through its influence transforming humanity from within and making it new' (Pope Paul VI, *Evangelii Nuntiandi*). We have to ask the question whether what we are creating frees people for that task or distracts them from it. There is no need for an artificial aid to unity where the altar is the focal point.

The Clergy

In the catholic tradition, we would still wish to refer to 'priestly forma-tion' and to keep the understanding that ordination is not simply the authority to perform certain tasks, but the giving of what Vatican II refers to as 'an indelible character'. We must also be aware of a worldly tendency to despise words such as 'authority', 'hierarchy' and 'obedience'. If collaborative ministry in mission involves only a democratic process in which all views are equal and no one has 'authority', then it is not true to the Gospel, as John Moore has shown in the previous section. We must redeem such words to our missionary life, for after all the New Testament makes much of the obedience of Jesus Christ to the will of the Father. Marion Mort speaks of this in her reflection on the Trinity later in this paper. If there is true collaborative ministry in mission, then there will be more demanded of the priest, particularly in the proper exercise of authority.

The Laity

'Their primary and immediate task is not to establish and develop the ecclesial community - this is the specific role of the pastors - but to put to use every Christian and evangelical possibility latent but already present and active in the affairs of the world. Their own field of evangelising activity is the vast and complicated world of politics, society and economics, but also the world of culture, of the sciences and the arts, of international life, of the mass media. It also includes other realities which are open to evangelization, such as human love, the family, the education of children and adolescents, professional work, suffering. The more Gospel-inspired lay people there are engaged in these realities, really involved in them, competent to promote them and conscious that they must exercise to the full their Christian powers which are often buried and suffocated, the more these realities will be at the service of the Kingdom of God and therefore salvation in Jesus Christ, without in any way losing or sacrificing their human content but rather pointing to a transcendent dimension which is often disregarded' (*Evangelii Nuntiandi*).

Spirituality

The life of prayer has to provide the foundation upon which all seek to fulfil their baptismal vocation. Even when individual members of the Church are apart, prayer is a source of their unity. Only those who know the presence of God in the whole of their lives can recognise his presence in the lives of others. Only those seeking to live a life of real holiness can truly witness to the love of God. Only those who are open to God in prayer can recognise his will for them. In this sense, then, priest and people are joined in a collaborative effort grounded in prayer, out of which must emerge a spirituality sufficient to the individual and to his or her circumstances, as St Francis de Sales says: '. . . it must be adapted to their particular strength, circumstance and duties'. In this way then, collaborative ministry in mission between clergy and laity must be grounded in prayer and worship and worked out and expressed in particular gifts and ministries.

Part Four

Examples

In this section, we offer some actual examples of collaborative ministry in practice. In doing so, we offer examples of different kinds relating to a variety of situations. Most of these situations relate directly to parochial ministry, but it should be remembered that there are also many more ways of working collaboratively. Although we have looked principally for 'good practice', we have also taken care to point up the problems and difficulties which have been faced by those taking up collaborative ministry in mission. Not all the examples we give are likely to exist in this form forever, and are likely to change, -at best they are snapshots of the possible. Nonetheless, we think that these examples have the potential to speak to those who may be trying to work out how best to work collaboratively in mission in their own situation and we hope they may prove helpful as visions of what can be achieved in the ministry for mission in the Church of England today and tomorrow.

A vision

Background

The parish is a 'township' of about 12,500 people which was originally a mining community in the north. The mine has now disappeared, robbing the community not only of its employment, but also of its way of life. There are four paid members of staff including a parish evangelist who was a lay person when he came, but who is now ordained, and a full-time youth leader.

A former incumbent of this parish felt his role is to be that of a visionary. It was he who drew the overall picture which individuals then have filled in. Only the outsider view can give this overall picture, the locals are too close to the situation to see it, though they may know their individual piece better than anyone. His role was further to release people to fulfil their potential in this way. He saw himself as an apostle sent in by the wider church to the local church, since although the local community may know the situation better than any outsider their church experience is necessarily limited. Delegation away from the centre is necessary, however, since the work could not happen if he had to do it himself. Consequently, he was required to trust and empower his people and this is what to him, charismatic renewal really means, allowing natural talents to flower and come forth.

Lay involvement

During the time of this incumbent the process of collaborative ministry and the growth in the church happened fairly slowly. Teams of lay people were established who have a substantial ministry. People from the churches run an ecumenical craft centre for the unemployed, 9-5 every weekday, who witness not only to the unemployed but also to the unemployable. Other church members also run a second hand clothes shop during the day and on Thursday night run a project to which they invite the contacts made at the shop. Therefore what they do combines evangelism with social concern. A team of Christians on the estate are responsible for a church plant which has a worship service on Monday nights. They are responsible for visiting, pastoral care and much of the service with its informal music.

The main church congregation was split into four, such that there tend to be separate congregations for each of the services on Sunday. The 9.30am Holy Communion tends to attract the older members, the 11.15am Special tends to be all age worship, the 6.30pm has a broader spectrum of all ages and the 8.30pm is a youth service. For each congregation there is a welcome pastor who looks out for and welcomes newcomers, and a ministry pastor who is available to help and pray with people after the service. 5-6 leaders are being trained up, while musical talent is emerging and being fed into a worship group. There is lay representation on the school's Board of Governors and a church person on the planning group for the pit centre redevelopment. This is important, because it is the laity, not the vicar, who have time to use these roles as evangelistic opportunities.

Problems

When people get into their roles, they become possessive of their own bits and this can be problematic. It is sometimes difficult to find things for new people to do without treading on other's toes. Therefore the priest must be on the lookout for entry points and sensitive to opportunity. There is also a problem with maintaining high standards. The flower festival was stopped because the level of expertise could not be maintained. It is difficult for people to see how other parts of the mechanism function and sometimes they don't appreciate what other people are doing. The whole process therefore needs to be kept fluid; it must not solidify. People need to be allowed to get over the feeling that they could not possibly do as well as the vicar who has been trained to fulfil particular functions. There needs to be a groundwork of trust on all sides, so as not to lead anyone astray. The philosophy that the church should serve the community is all very well in theory, but the working out of it tends to be uncertain.

Vision

The parish seeks to catch the vision that is represented in Isaiah: individuals, community and the land is itself restored. Now, the pit-centre is being developed, so there is indeed redevelopment and restoration and this helps to make concrete the theological picture.

Ministry team development

The Team in question consists of eight churches in villages in a diocese in the south east. The Team working across the Group consists of two stipendiary priests and three readers. But in one parish, a village of some 500 people, with a church two miles from the centre of the community, the life and ministry of the Church has been developed and sustained by a lay ministry team consisting of:

> Worship leader
> Group leaders
> Those responsible for pastoral care, counselling, children's
>   work and ministry of healing

The role of the two stipendiary clergy has been to develop and steer this lay team and to train the leaders for their different ministry tasks.

Priorities in the life of the church are outreach, teaching and prayer that leads to a personal commitment. Much emphasis is placed on friendship, counselling and the study of scripture. In seven years the average attendance at worship has grown from 4 to 90+. The church also draws from the surrounding villages as people hear of its life and vitality. Children and teenagers make up a third of the congregation. All ages are brought together using a family service. When the children are taken out, the adults present have the opportunity for serious teaching.

The growth of the church has been fostered by a group of lay people who, through prayer and bible study, have sought to be guided by the Holy Spirit. During the past two years, following a parish weekend attended by over a hundred people, house groups have been formed. Regular 'basics' courses are run. The church draws from the wider village community as people hear of its life and vitality. Fresh faces are regularly seen at Sunday worship when there is always a small group ready to offer friendship and counselling.

The vision for the future is to develop lay ministry in the other seven parishes, which may not necessarily follow the same model. These parishes, which have a more traditional approach to ministry, are currently at different stages of development.

There are basically two problems which tend to inhibit ministry development in the more traditional parishes:

–   emotional and intellectual difficulties which are sometimes reflected in (a) a fear of change and a desire to hold on to traditional patterns and structures of ministry and (b) an inability or unwillingness to relate faith to life.

–   the unavailability of people in small communities, both in terms of numbers and time, who have vision and/or leadership potential for Ministry Teams.

Getting a team going

St L. is a parish of just under 7,000 people in the north west of England. The area is classified as suburban/rural and comprises a mixture of 1930s council housing, 1950s private housing and a number of dwellings ranging from miners' cottages to detached villas. The parish does in fact stem from an old mining and farming community and with five farms in operation still maintains much of that ethos. The parish church, like most of the community it serves, tends to be traditional and conservative, although much change has taken place over the last ten years. The church has a usual sunday attendance of 200+ adults, together with the usual organisations. There are on average 60 baptisms, 50 funerals and 28 weddings per year. One important factor affecting the ministry at St L. is that fact that the vicar is senior chaplain to a large 500+ bed hospital situated in the parish which takes up a considerable amount of his time.

For a number of years, discussions had taken place with the Bishop regarding the possibility of full time assistant staff at St L.. By 1991, when it finally became apparent that this was not going to happen, the real opportunities for developing a local ministry team, – a group of people, lay and ordained, to act as leaders in the church, – began to present itself. At the Church's Annual General Meeting in April 1992 a scheme was presented based on diocesan guidelines. The main principles were that:

a.   the team should consist of men and women of all ages and should comprise laity, lay readers and clergy.

b.   selection of the team and its work should be under the auspices of the PCC.

c.   the work of the team would be task oriented, each task or ministry identified by the PCC.

d.   the individuals would be chosen to a particular task or ministry.

e.   the team should make a major annual report to the PCC.

f.   the life of the team should be based in prayer.

g.   as far as possible, the team, including the vicar, should develop a shared ministry concept.

In October 1992, the team was selected and training began in November. The training was for the most part team training loosely based on the GUML (Group for Urban Ministry and Leadership) scheme which had been in operation for some time. Although the team felt the need to be trained together, much of the material used for GUML was not found to be suitable for a Local Ministry Team where the issues were clearly different. Nonetheless, the team training was seen on the whole to be very valuable and has facilitated the team in bonding together in mutual support of ministry and development of individual and corporate spirituality.

The team was formally commissioned by a suffragan bishop of the diocese in October 1993, and has spent some time identifying specific ministries and roles within the parish. The major issues which it has tackled so far have included financial development to meet the sudden considerable rise in demand faced by so many today. A complete redevelopment of all aspects of Christian nurture and work with young people, in collaboration with other churches and agencies in the area has been demanded. The first stages in development of social responsibility and major moves in adult Christian education and development for leadership, including lay readership, lay leadership and Local Non-Stipendiary Ministry.

There is no doubt that with sole responsibility for a busy parish and his hospital duties, the vicar would have found it very difficult to develop even one of these areas of concern. By the training and development of the Local Ministry Team a number of ministries and developments have become possible and it has provided a real opportunity for the church to exploit all its human resources to the best result. It is as yet early days for this Local Ministry Team, but it believes itself to be in the vanguard of total church ministry for the next century.

A church centre in an Urban Priority Area

Background

The parish church is a small church situated in what is left of a village, but attached to a large estate, which was, in the seventies and early eighties one of the most notorious of outer housing UPAs in the north west. At that time, the church was of the catholic tradition and very run down with very little lay involvement. Since then, the church has adopted to evangelical thinking and practice and the ancient church has been completely reorganised as a church centre. This, in tandem with government and CUF money, has seen an upturn in the estate's fortunes, and a new style of ministry in which the laity have come to play a much greater part. There is a vicar, a curate and an NSM.

Lay involvement – Church

There are two lay readers and laity participate fully in the worship which is based on teaching and choruses, but is not charismatic. There are also prayer teams who are available to lead prayers at the end of the service. There are six house-groups, some of which are lay-led.

Lay involvement – social

Laity from the church run a coffee bar, a mothers and toddlers group, a pensioner's lunchclub, lunches after the Wednesday Communion, and a latchkey club for schoolchildren. A volunteer is available to give advice on welfare rights in the church centre twice a week. There is usually something going on every day and there has been a marked improvement in participation by the estate.

Growth

Outreach possibilities have been especially discovered in the occasional offices. There are large numbers of weddings and funerals and because there has been a strict baptism policy, a large number of 'blessings'. This means that a large number of unchurched people are coming into the Centre (at one 'blessing' at least 80 of the 176 congregation were visitors) and this provides the church laity with evangelistic opportunities. The main problem faced by the minister at the time of change of direction was the lack of confidence and a reluctance to be involved, but this was overcome by isolating tasks which people could cope with. Estate people may not feel that they can articulate their faith easily, but many cook meals and feel confident about being available to provide lunches. There has been encouragement for those lacking confidence. Above all, the change from peripheral church to church *centre* has been important rather than anything to do with the change of churchmanship.

Collaboration in planting a church

Background

The parish consists of two churches and covers an area of the working-class part of a seaside town in the south, which has a large proportion of evangelical churches offering a Bible-based ministry. The population tends to shift around these churches, choosing which they find suits them and the parish church tends to attract people, including from the free churches. The population of the parish is about 22,000 people. It has called itself a traditional, evangelical church. There are three clergy. There is one church council and a church committee for administration.

Church plant

The parish church's congregation grew so large, it was necessary to plant a church. This took place after consultation between clergy and laity about how to cope with the overspill. The new church is planted in a non-permanent building which is hired, there are no overheads. Originally 24 people went, then 48, and the average congregation is 70. It is particularly attractive to young families. Although the church plant is potentially independent, efforts have been made to ensure it does not go off at a tangent. The church plant is not as free as the parish church. The PCC still holds the plant within its structure and it is bound by team policy, although there is an area of autonomy within which the plant can make its own decisions. Although there is clerical oversight, little is led by the clergy at the church plant. Baptism and wedding preparation takes place in house groups. People who had been unable to express their gifts at the parish church have found new opportunities at the church plant. For example, door to door visiting is resisted at the parish church, but feels entirely right around the plant. Also musical talents have found a place at the plant and the style of worship has become charismatic, with healing and expression of gifts. Lay readers are given a job description and a chance for an annual review of their achievements with the clergy. There is a co-ordinator system giving details of who is responsible to whom. This operates within a five year aim which is reviewed yearly.

Drawbacks

When the church was planted, the parish church experienced a time of difficulty because the people who went tended to be the senior leaders eg the church warden and young people's leader. The leadership base at the parish church was weakened, leading to hardship, sadness and loss. The parish church has therefore had to regroup and consolidate to regain its leadership base. It has therefore affected the role of the Team Rector, who had to concentrate on maintaining stability at the parish church. Another particular problem is that the laity are all volunteers, while the clergy are paid. This raises difficulties with asking for and maintaining commitment.

The church plant has had to face questions about what kind of clerical oversight is most appropriate and how it can be sustained. It was felt to be unfair to put a curate in the first year of ministry into such a situation. The plant has had to decide what kind of worship is most appropriate and ideally wished to be ecumenical, but there were special difficulties with the turnover of free church ministers and the inability of other denominations to provide money.

Your Kingdom Come, a church as 'oasis in the desert'

The church

St G. was consecrated in 1814 and has been the centre of a worshipping Anglican community for over 180 years. Its unique cast iron structures has drawn many visitors over the years and it is a Grade I listed building. Recently the church has undergone extensive refurbishment, with an office, toilet and kitchen and meeting rooms added which blend with the interior.

The Community

Once set in the midst of an affluent community, this church has seen a dramatic change since it was consecrated. St G. is now set in the middle of an inner city Urban Priority Area and is home for a strong community facing problems of unemployment, with a high percentage of council houses, private landlords and elderly people.

The church, however, has stood the test of time and is seen as an 'oasis in the desert'.

Church community

During its history, the church community has also changed dramatically and the churchmanship has changed from catholic to open evangelical. There are 108 people on the electoral roll, of which 70+ are women. Sunday worship is mainly attended by women, with fewer men, but a good percentage of young people. There is one male incumbent, one female associate priest, two male readers and one male reader in training. There is a second GUML team in training made up of five women and four men.

1986 saw the introduction of a GUML team at St G. After much discussion, prayer and teaching it was agreed (with some reservations!) that a team should be formed. Originally consisting of three men and four women, the team began its journey of learning together. At first none of the members was sure about their part in the team, but soon a strong bond between them was formed and enabled the members to be honest and truthful with each other. This honesty and love was nonetheless sometimes painful, especially where the team as a whole would say sometimes yes to an individual's ideas and hopes and sometimes no. During the process of team building, the team members shared with each other what they felt they were called to do and the team shared and nurtured this calling.

This team's seven year term is now at an end and a new GUML team is in training. The development and commitment to the local community has been strengthened, and it can be said that GUML has produced vision within the church: a vision of 'inside out' and 'outside in', with provision for the building reorganisation and a new willingness to pray 'Your Kingdom come here in St G. as it is in Heaven'. .

Catholic collaboration

Background

The parish consists of 4,000 people and is situated on a hill-top overlooking the valleys containing big West Yorkshire towns. It is rural, with some industry (stone-quarrying) but surrounded by urban scenes. Its housing is a mixture of older stock, private homes and housing estates.

Worship

The parish is in the catholic tradition and its worship is eucharistic. Laity read and give the intercessions and are as involved as far as the Eucharist allows; however there has been in recent years the introduction of an informal Sunday Evening Service in order to attract those who might be put off by the formality of the Eucharist People with musical talents have been building up a music group and this is lay-led.

The house group has been closed in order to concentrate on other things, especially since the parish has had great success in mission ventures. Outreach events have been run by laity, while the incumbent has merely kept 'a watchful eye'. The parish had experienced a spiritual renewal under another incumbent and part of his brief was to move into 'new areas of growth and outreach'.

The first major event was a Mission in which 100 churches participated. Led by a team from Oxford, it included the parish church. The incumbent was on the management committee of the whole event and was therefore tied up, so the parish's own individual input was entirely lay-led. They put on a major arts festival on a Sunday, which was described as a 'mini-Greenbelt'. They had a range of music from traditional to rock in the church and the premises opposite. The theme was feeding the five thousand and was very successful, attracting 2,000 people. It had been advertised very widely and raised the profile of the church in the parish. The laity showed great enterprise and initiative but agreed that this also had a cost, especially where some people strongly disagreed with the project.

As a follow-up to this, the parish also ran a 'Sunrise' project on adult baptism between Easter and Pentecost. It concentrated on those who had perhaps missed out on baptism in infancy and offered a second chance. The laity sent out questionnaires and visited designated areas. They also showed great imagination in putting together a video, written by the laity, featuring local places and in which people talk about Christianity. This is now valued as a resource for baptism visits. This culminated in an open-air ecumenical service at Pentecost with the possibility for open air baptisms, and a challenge to the people in the crowd to perform a major act of renewal. The water of a swimming pool was blessed and they were encouraged, in renewing baptismal vows to take the water in their hands. This was a very dramatic and moving occasion, and six adults were baptised as a result of the project.

In this parish important ideas from evangelical roots have been translated into catholic practice and as this has happened, mission opportunities in collaboration have arisen. The view which has emerged is that collaboration between clergy and laity in the catholic tradition has great dramatic potential in outreach, that catholic Anglicans are good at marching with banners; they have incense to swing and holy water to sprinkle. This need not be mere ceremony, but is first eye-catching and then dynamic.

Some lay people in the parish felt that some catholic parishes convince themselves that collaboration for outreach and evangelism are incompatible with their churchmanship but that this parish demonstrates that nothing could be further from the truth.

A religious community

In this example, a small number of sisters from a religious community left the mother house in the south to travel to a northern town. As a religious community, the sisters collaborated among themselves in order closely to become a pattern of the Body of Christ. The sisters preferred to meet as a group, to thrash out ideas for their work, to make mistakes and try again. In this way the impetus for loving and learning is continuous.

The sisters felt called to move to the north and to be touched by the experience of the area. They resisted going into a traditional parish setting and would not set themselves any specific task, role or expectations, but decided to concentrate on their corporate life, prayer and worship, and endeavour to discern what might be happening. Again, a sense of vision was sought, since the sisters were initially uncertain whether to wait until people asked something of them or to begin initiatives themselves.

What people *did* ask, was to share the sisters' prayer life and they came in off the streets to the daily offices. There were also particular contacts and relationships in the neighbourhood. The house was in a terrace and from this the neighbourly contact spread.

The sisters had two particularly important sets of contacts and collaborative relationships which they felt have been brought about by their gender. The first was with the Islamic community. They found they had unique access to Muslim homes through initial contacts with women and children, especially because of the way they are dressed. Further, aspects of their religious life: their prayers, their vows of obedience, their preparation for the offices, struck a chord with women who understand about prayer and ritual cleanliness. This has given the sisters particular opportunities to work with this part of the community. In particular, they have been able to exchange important religious ideas about food and the holiness of the kitchen, in a way not possible for others to understand. It is noticeable that the clergy know themselves to be excluded from these contacts. The sisters were able to visit the Mosque and many of the women and children visited the house and talked about the crucifix and the tabernacle of the reserved sacrament by finding analogies. The sisters felt this was a very special and precious relationship, which was not based on mere information exchange, but on shared religious experience. They therefore feel they have a particular opportunity to bring about collaboration at the inter-faith level.

The second set of contacts was with prostitutes in the red light district. Here, they felt they are able to keep a distance born of their different sexual status which paradoxically allowed the women to come close to them without feeling compromised or in danger of losing their identity. The community can therefore fill a gap where the agencies cannot go and that the sisters sensitively and instinctively isolate what is required. In this way they were able to form partnerships which sustained the wider church without compromising the integrity of any of the parties.

A Local Ecumenical Partnership

This Local Ecumenical Partnership is situated in a modern village, population 5,000, in East Anglia. The church is sponsored by five denominations (Baptist, Church of England, Methodist, Society of Friends, United Reformed church) and has a local covenant with a Roman Catholic congregation who use the building.

An active membership of 190 results in an average adult morning congregation of around 150 but there is an extensive 'fringe' and a reasonably steady turnover with people being drawn into the church through outreach initiatives on the one hand and established folk moving out of the village on the other.

The main leadership body is the Church Council which is made up of the Executive Committee (which deals with the practical side of church life) and the Ministry Team (which has oversight of worship and overall spiritual direction as well as pastoral matters). The church staff are ex officio members of the Ministry Team and look to the minister to provide a central leadership role within the context of the team approach. There is a well-organised and centralised system of Homegroups and these provide forums for learning, prayer, fellowship and pastoral care in manageable units. Other pastoral teams exist to cater for particular needs.

The church has been in interregnum for over a year but the worship and work of the Christian body has continued to develop and there is currently an excitement about things that are happening on a spiritual level. Ministerial work has been shared between the remaining full time member of staff (a 'lay assistant') and others in lay leadership. Worship has been led by lay preachers and ordained ministers attached to the congregation with visiting ministers being welcomed from time to time. It is recognised that there is a need for a minister to give time to the wider church and to the wider community and to provide 'a focus for leadership and unity' in the Christian body in the long term but we have discovered that God provides for our needs and equips lay people as necessary for effectively negotiating a short term period without a minister. We believe strongly in every member ministry and that we all have a part to play in the church operating effectively to God's glory.

The experience here, both with and without a minister, is that leadership and pastoral care are ideally shared between ordained and lay, men and women, between those working full-time for the church and those who give time outside secular employment. This experience affirms the need for focused leadership, the need for that leadership to be shared and the need for every Christian to be motivated and equipped for ministry in the church and in the world.

An example from the world church

The people of the hill tribes in the interior of S. are animists. The strategy of the Anglican Interior Mission is to seek the conversion of the headmen of the villages; once the headman is baptised, the whole village is baptised with him; whatever the headman's religion is, so it is for all his people. The village is then instructed in the Christian faith. As in the Acts of the Apostles, instruction follows baptism.

Lay leadership is essential to the process. Even if it were right to leave evangelism to the clergy, there would not be enough of them. So the diocese has a well-established programme to identify and train young leaders.

When students complete their fifth form school exams, they must wait three months to learn the results. The diocese offers them an opportunity to participate in an intense training programme, and then the opportunity to work in congregations, under the supervision of a priest, as lay youth workers for this period. Those who do not decide to go for further study toward their A levels can receive more training and are then assigned to a congregation for two more years, again under the supervision of a priest. At the end of this time a few young people may be encouraged to go on for further study and to begin the process leading to ordination. These people enter a three-year work-study programme that involves six months in a congregation and six months of study each year.

A new centre, capable of accommodating a large number of people, has already been opened in the middle of the country.

Visitors to the diocese are greatly impressed by the way these young lay leaders, both women and men, minister to their congregations. Their spiritual maturity in leading worship, which may include responsibility for the whole service, is a major factor in the growth of the church, both spiritually and in membership.

(adapted from *Renew Our Vision in Evangelism*, published for the Mission Issues and Strategy Advisory Group of the Anglican Consultative Council, 1991)

A Checklist
for Collaborative Ministry in Mission

How to recognise it when you see it

Revd Peter Bradley

There will be:

- a high level of communication, not only within the church congregation but also between the church and the parish

- a ministry of welcome involving clergy and laity

- input into the life of the church from all directions, not a reliance upon the faithful few

- shared purpose, aims and objectives

- evidence of consultation and joint decision making

- desire for growth in understanding

- lay participation in worship and planning worship

- wide recognition of skills and limitations

- identification and deployment of a variety of ministries and communicating with developments not only within the church but also within the parish

- some form of accountability and appraisal of those ministries

- staff meetings involving clergy, Readers and lay leaders

- a similar quality of input from laity into church as into 'work'

- a desire to do more

- a high level of trust and tolerance

- flexibility

- openness to change

- allowing initiatives

- minimum interference from clergy
- evidence of people being valued
- space and scope for personal growth, including staff development and professional growth
- mutual enablement
- laity involved in pastoral work and for this to be acceptable within the parish
- a focus of pastoral work and for this to be acceptable within the parish
- a focus of pastoral care located away from the parsonage house
- appointment of a secretary or administrator
- clergy who don't attempt to fill every breach in times of crisis
- productive ways in which the Body heals itself, including agreed conflict resolution procedures

Source: The Revd Canon Tony Chesterman, In Service Training Officer, Diocese of Derby

RESOURCES

Group for Urban Leadership and Ministry
c/o Board of Ministry
Diocese of Liverpool

Local Ministry Teams Advisory Group

address as above
Diocesan Strategies:
The Future: A Strategy for the Diocese of Canterbury, 1994, especially part 2, Ministry
Report to the Portsmouth Diocesan Pastoral Committee of a working party on *Patterns of Ministry*

Diocese of Bath and Wells: *Deanery Chapter Collaborative Ministry Programme*

A Devotional Postscript

An image of the Trinity

Mrs Marion Mort

Our discussions of collaborative ministry in mission began with reference to the Trinity. In reflection on what has been said by my fellow-contributors on collaborative ministry in mission, we may seek to move from an abstract idea of Trinity, to an image: the Rublev Icon. The illustration on the front cover of this booklet is a contemporary artist's re-working of the icon image, and it may be helpful to use this as a focus.

If we attempt to visualise Trinity, we may well imagine a stained glass representation of a cloud-surrounded Father God above an impossibly hovering dove above a crucifix held rigidly vertical in a narrow lancet. The Rublev Icon, however, dissolves this hierarchical structure and presents us with an image of unity, harmony and courtesy, in which no-one is dominant, even if the icon protects the sense that the Son and the Holy Spirit proceed from the Father. If we allow this image to influence our prayer, reflection and meditation, we can begin to recognise within it the eternal activity of the Trinity, mutually loving, interdependent, harmonious, indivisible but yet three identifiable persons in one God, each with a distinctive part in terms of the whole of God's self-revelation of his loving purposes towards humanity and the whole created order. As the Proper Preface for Trinity Sunday in the Book of Common Prayer Communion Service says: '. . . one God, one Lord; not one only Person, but three Persons in one Substance. For that which we believe of the glory of the Father, the same we believe of the Son, and of the Holy Ghost, without any difference or inequality'. It is surely an attractive model.

If collaboration in mission has to do with labouring together on a common task and if ministry is about service offered not only to the community, but also to one another and to the world then there is some encouragement to look to the life and activity of the Trinity in so far as we can discern or imagine it as offering some significant pattern or model by which we may be guided.

The persons of the Trinity never act at variance with one another. They work together for the Good. There is no struggle for precedence. It is impossible to withdraw or abstract one member from the Trinity whose Unity is definitive. To try and imagine one without the other two is impossible. The relationship of Father, Son and Spirit and the manner by which we identify them (for example: Life-giver, Pain-bearer, Love-maker) is of mutuality and inter-dependence and of abundant, overflowing love. The image of the Rublev Icon offers us the courteous inclination and attentiveness of the three figures to one another. This is a company that listens as well as speaks, that shares silence as well as conversation, that reflects together on the action that has been taken and which will be taken together.

If we then withdraw from the inner space of the icon, we may remember that it is properly called 'The Hospitality of Abraham'. Out of a model of eternal Trinity, we discover a model of human activity. The hospitality of Abraham as he entertained the angels unawares is proffered modestly, but he and Sarah offer of their best. What do we learn here? Through sharing and through offering, the guest becomes the host and gives the gift of life: Sarah will bear a son (Genesis 18:1-10). So at Emmaus, the giver of the Word becomes the recipient of the words of invitation. By such invitation, the unrecognised guest becomes the host who is known in the breaking of the bread as the one who brings life and hope (Luke 24:13-35). By sharing, new gifts are known, new possibilities are created. Word and sacrament, high priest and laity are all here.

We are invited to share in Christ's ministry of reconciliation. Our ministry, then, is shared from the beginning. But that in which we share is one, a totality. We may then understand that there is no question of there being a ministry that is broken up into bits wherein the bits have no reference to one another:'I only do this and you only do that'. Nor is such a ministry delegated:'You may do this or that, but I reserve the authority to myself'.

We can understand this better by reference back to the distinctiveness of the persons of the Trinity, who are yet not rigidly delineated by their function or activity. For example, we are used to designating the Father as Creator, the Son as Redeemer and the Spirit as Comforter and Sustainer. But we see the Spirit of God moving over the face of the waters at the Creation, while both John 1 and Colossians speak in swirling terms of Christ not only as the firstborn of all creation but active in it. 'All things were made by him and without him was not anything made that was made' (John 1:3). In the first letter of John Jesus

Christ the Son of God is described as 'an advocate [Parakleton] with the Father' (I John, 2:1), but in John's Gospel it is Christ who says 'I will pray the Father and he will send you another Advocate'(John 14:16). We may also remember that the Orthodox do not celebrate Trinity Sunday separately, but at Pentecost with the coming of the Holy Spirit. The Spirit is often seen as the agent of renewal and is invoked for the renewal of the whole creation and for the renewal of the Church. We may assume then, as we are made in God's image, that our individual natures do not preclude us from any kind of ministry within any part of our common mission. Rather it is our individual choices, understandings and sense of vocation, which lead us to particular opportunities for ministry in mission.

How then do we discern what these choices, understanding and vocation might be? In scripture, prayer precedes ministry. Jesus looks up to heaven, he prays, he gives thanks, he heals, before he feeds, before he raises from the dead. So all ministry and all collaborative ministry for mission, must surely be grounded in prayer. We must be open to God and to the movement of the Spirit in order to discern our distinctive contribution to that which is both whole and His.

So in Acts, the Apostles pray before appointing, before sending, before deciding. The choosing of those for the ministry of distribution, humdrum though that service may appear, is itself dependent on discernment, praying and commissioning. The deacons collaborate with the Apostles and with the whole Household of Faith in order that the Apostles should have time to teach, and so that the hungry are fed (Acts 6: 1-7). In this way the life of the Church is sustained in all its aspects. It is surely significant that the Apostles invite the people who have identified the need, to choose the deacons from among themselves, indicating that they should be of good repute, full of the Holy Spirit and wisdom. Even though the practical side of their ministry is waiting at table, it is recognised as important, – and the Apostles pray and lay hands on them just as they did when sending out missionaries. Significantly, the verse that follows the story of their commissioning reads:'And the word of God increased and the disciples multiplied greatly in Jerusalem and a great many priests were obedient to the faith'. What does this tell us first about the relationship between mission and pastoral care? Second, what does this tell us about the nature of obedience: that it is not subservience, or submission to dominance but acting in a profound understanding of the common task for the greater good. There is a missiological understanding of obedience which is profoundly significant for the practice of collaborative ministry:

> Now there are varieties of gifts, but the same Spirit;
> and there are varieties of service but the same Lord;
> and there are varieties of working, but it is the same God
> who inspires them all in everyone. To each is given the
> manifestation of the Spirit for the common Good. (1 Cor 12: 4-7)

Ministry, whether from the Lord's table or ours, is significant, because it is a sign, a sacrament, an icon of the outpoured love of God for all creation.

If the quality of collaboration is to reflect the relationships we perceive within the Trinity and if it is to be true to the model that Paul offers us in 1 Corinthians, then it must be collaborative in its conception as well as in its life. 'Let us pray' followed by 'let us . . . together' is the way forward, rather than 'I have decided . . . will you . . . ?'

LIST OF BOOKS QUOTED AND OTHER USEFUL BOOKS

Boff, Leonardo, *Ecclesiogenesis: The Base Communities Reinvent the Church*, Maryknoll, New York, Orbis Books, 1986

Breaking New Ground: Church Planting in the Church of England, CHP 1994

Cooper, Norman P, *Collaborative Ministry: Communion, Contention, Commitment*, Gracewing, 1993

Faith in the City: A Call for Action by Church and Nation, CHP, 1985

Faith in the Countryside, ACORA 1990

Good News in Our Times, the Gospel and Our Culture, CHP 1991

Greenwood, Robin, *Transforming Priesthood*, SPCK 1994

eds Napier, Charles and Hamilton-Brown, Jimmy, *A New Workbook on Rural Evangelism*, especially *Collaboration in Action*, pp. 55-71, Parish and People 1994; Parish and People also have produced other booklets which cover collaborative working, eg *Working Together in Teams and Groups*, by John Hammersley 1989. Contact Parish and People, The Old Mill, Spetisbury, Blandford Forum, Dorset, DT11 9DF

Pope Paul VI, *Evangelii Nuntiandi*

Sofield, Loughlan, *Collaborative Ministry: Skills and Guidelines*, Ave Maria Press, 1987

Taylor, John V, *The Go-Between God: The Holy Spirit and Christian Mission*, London SCM Press 1972

Team and Group Ministries: A Report by the Ministry Co-ordinating Group (GS 660) 1985

The Sign we Give, Report from the Working Party on Collaborative Ministry, Bishops' Conference of England and Wales, 1995

Tiller, John, *A Strategy for the Church's Ministry*, CIO Publishing 1983

Turning the Sod, A Workbook for Multi-Parish Benefices, available from The Revd Jeremy Martineau, Arthur Rank Centre, Stoneleigh Park, Warwickshire, CV8 2LZ